My Pretty Princess
Beauty Kit and Book

Written by Lisa Telford

Photography by Top That! Studio

Printed in Hong Kong   First Edition   10 9 8 7 6 5 4 3 2

Library of Congress Catalog Card Number: 2003091340

ISBN 0-7868-5924-5

For more Disney Press fun, visit www.disneybooks.com

Contents

Off to the Ball!

What's more fun than getting together with your friends, sharing beauty secrets, and trying them out on each other? What princess-at-heart can resist sparkling gems, glittering tiaras, pretty hair accessories, and fun nail polish colors? The Disney Princesses have gotten together to share their beauty secrets and tips with you. It's your very own private makeover session with Ariel, Snow White, Jasmine, Cinderella, Sleeping Beauty, and Belle. In this book you'll learn all about hair and nail care, as well as stunning hairstyles fit for a princess. You and your friends will have hours of fun re-creating the princesses' styles as well as finding your own look.

And remember—get permission from an adult to use all the accessories in the beauty kit, especially the nail polish. (But don't worry, unlike regular nail polish, it comes off very easily.)

Hair Fit for a Princess

You don't have to live in a palace or spend a fortune to have really royal hair. Just follow these simple hair-care tips.

Shampoo

Obviously, you'll need shampoo to wash your hair. Choose which type you buy carefully. Most girls only need to use a gentle shampoo made for normal hair.

If you wash your hair every day, use a special shampoo made for frequent use. You may want to add a little water to the shampoo in your hand before you lather up.

A Tip from Sleeping Beauty

Don't always use the same shampoo. You may need to try a different kind during the warm summer months. If you swim a lot, use a shampoo that will protect your hair from chlorine. In the winter, your hair may feel dry from the heat inside and the chilly weather outside. If this is the case, you may want to use a shampoo for dry hair or try a deep conditioner.

Conditioner

You should condition your hair after washing, or every other day if daily conditioning makes it too oily.

Long hair is more likely to need conditioner than short hair. And dry hair needs a creamier conditioner than oily hair.

Styling Products

For special styles, you can try hair mousse or gel.

Only use a medium-sized dab (the size of an egg) of mousse on the roots of damp hair before you blow-dry it.

Use gel for a sleeker look on damp or dry hair, and to create spiky styles.

A Tip from Belle

Check the instructions before you buy a conditioner. Some of them should be rinsed out after one or two minutes. Others are "leave-in" conditioners that you don't rinse out. If you have straight, fine hair, these "leave-in" conditioners may weigh it down. This will make your hair hard to style.

A Tip from Ariel

If you use lots of hair products, especially hair spray, use a shampoo that is especially designed to clean the products out of your hair. If you don't, the products will build up in your hair and make it look dull. And you can't be as pretty as a princess with dull hair!

Hairbrushes

If you style your hair a lot, you will need two different brushes: a flat one and a round one. Use the flat one to brush your hair, and a round one to create different styles when blow-drying your hair. If you have curly hair, you can scrunch it between your fingers to dry it, but you'll still need to get rid of any knots with a comb.

Combs

Wide-toothed combs work well to get knots out of wet hair. Use a narrow-toothed comb to keep your ponytail neat and to make a zigzag part.

A Tip from Snow White

When you go on vacation to a warm place, try to find a style that doesn't require much blow-drying. After being in the sun all day, your hair needs a break from the heat.

Accessories

You can make short hair look even prettier with hair clips and hair swirls, especially the ones included in the beauty kit.

For longer hair, you'll need an assortment of hair elastics and probably some hairpins.

Pretty hair clips with flowers or other designs are great for holding twisted hair in place, and keeping hair out of your face.

Curling and Straightening

If you want curls, you can use a curling iron, rollers, or a hot brush.

If you want straight hair, try a straightening iron.

NOTE: These heated hair tools can get very hot, so remember to ask an adult for help.

A Tip from Jasmine

Never use rubber bands to hold your hair in a ponytail or a braid. It will hurt when you take it out, but even worse, it can rip your hair and make it weak or frizzy.

Hair Dryer

If you have curly hair, you may want to use a diffuser. This will allow you to dry your hair without causing it to be frizzy.

Overdrying can make your hair dry or brittle. Whenever you can, let your hair dry naturally.

A Tip from Cinderella

If your hair is fine and flyaway, don't use a brush with plastic bristles—this will make it worse! Use a brush with natural bristles instead.

Hairdos (and Don'ts)

It's not always easy being a princess. But luckily, you are not alone! Here are some rules that the Disney Princesses follow in order to keep their hair looking its best.

Don't use heated hair tools every day. The heat will dry out your hair, make it frizzy, and create split ends.

Do try new styles and new ways of putting your hair up. Place your ponytail at the side, or high on your head, or low down where your hair meets your neck. Variety is the spice of life.

Don't expect miracles from your hair or from your hairdresser. Just like each princess, you have to find a hairstyle that's just right for you and your hair type.

Do keep all of your hair accessories clean and tidy. Brushes and combs, even hairpins and barrettes, should be cleaned regularly.

Do make the most of free product samples. Lots of magazines enclose small packets for you to try before you buy the product.

 Do go with your mom or your friends when they get their hair cut so you have the chance to see different hairstyles.

Don't try to save money by not going to the hair-dresser. As a general rule, short hair needs to be cut every four weeks; medium-length hair should be cut every six weeks; and long hair needs to be trimmed every eight weeks to keep the ends in good condition.

Don't blow-dry hair that is completely wet. Let your hair dry naturally for a few minutes, then blow it dry.

Do ask your hair-dresser questions about your hair. Ask which products would be good for your hairstyle. Or which styles work best with your hair type. Watch carefully when your hairdresser blow-dries your hair so you know what to do when you're styling it at home.

Don't waste money on hair products that you won't use. Just because your friend uses wet-look gel doesn't mean that it will look good in **your** hair.

Really Royal Nails

Cinderella does all the cleaning. Snow White cooks for the Seven Dwarfs, and Sleeping Beauty picks flowers and berries in the woods. How do the Disney Princesses keep their hands and nails looking so beautiful? Here are their secrets!

The main items you need for a really royal manicure are hand cream and a pack of emery boards. These are very inexpensive and you can buy them at the supermarket or a beauty-supply store.

Rule One

Always apply hand cream after washing your hands. Water makes your hands and nails dry out. And the hotter the water, the more damage it will do. The hand cream will control this by putting moisture back in your skin.

A Tip from Snow White

Keep your hands out of water as much as you can. Wear rubber gloves when you're cleaning to protect your hands and nails.

A Tip from Cinderella

Carry an emery board in your schoolbag in case you snag or break a nail. The one in the beauty kit should fit perfectly.

Rule Two

Never bite your nails. If you want to stop, try painting your nails with nail polish or putting on press-on nails. Painted nails look too nice to nibble! And press-on nails will not only prevent you from chewing on your own nails but will give them time to grow.

Rule Three

File your nails when they are dry. When your nails are wet, they are weaker, softer, and bend more easily. File your nails before you take a bath or shower.

A Tip from Sleeping Beauty

If your nails look stained, soak them in warm water with a few drops of lemon juice. Don't do this more than once a week, though, or it can weaken your nails.

A Tip from Ariel

Give your nails a break from nail polish every few days. If you wear it too often, your nails will become weak and may turn a yellowish color.

Rule Four

Learn the correct way to file your nails. Use an emery board, not a metal file, to smooth the edges. Hold the emery board at an angle. Then file each nail from the outer edge to the middle, one side at a time.

Nail Know-how

Make the most of your beautifully cared-for nails so that people notice them right away. Later in this book, each of the Disney Princesses will show you her favorite nail-painting secrets. But first, here are some basic rules for perfectly painted nails:

Base Coat

Whenever you paint your nails, start with a base coat—a clear polish that protects your nails from everything you paint on top. It's even more important to use a base coat if you paint your nails with dark colors, which can often stain your nails.

Colored Coat

This is the fun part—painting your nails with your favorite colors. Paint one even stroke in the center of your nail, from the bottom to the top. Paint a second stroke to fill in the space on one side, and a third stroke on the other side. Let the polish dry completely. You may want to apply a second coat to even out the color.

A Tip from Belle

If you can't wait for your nails to dry completely, wait until they are nearly dry, and then dip them in cold water for a minute. Be careful not to smudge them when you dry your hands.

A Tip from Jasmine

To avoid large blobs of nail polish, dip the brush partway into the bottle, then wipe some polish off on the inside edge of the bottle rim before you start to paint. If you make a mistake and get some polish on your fingers, dip a cotton swab into nail polish remover. Then carefully wipe the polish until it comes off.

Top Coat

When your colored polish is completely dry, paint a clear coat on top to make your nails shiny and glossy.

Pretty Press-on Nails

The pretty pink press-on nails in your beauty kit are a great shortcut to gorgeous hands. And the sticky pads make them easy to apply.

1. Wipe your nails with a cotton ball dipped in nail polish remover. This will take off any dirt or oil, which could prevent the press-on nails from sticking.

2. Gently buff your nails—if they are too smooth the sticky pads will slide off. Peel the sticky pads off the backing sheet and place one in the center of each nail.

3. One at a time, peel off the paper cover from the sticky pads, and put the press-on nails in place. Press down hard to make sure they will stay on.

4. If your press-on nails look too long, you can file them to the length you want. Do this before you put them on. Then you can add glitter nail polish, a new color, or leave them as they are.

Decorations

You can decorate your press-on nails with the stickers and gems included in the beauty kit. Nail stickers are really easy to apply. Just position your favorite ones right on your nails. Gems often have sticky backs, too, but can be difficult to get in place. Use tweezers to make sure they are exactly where you want them to be.

A Tip from Ariel

Don't shake your bottle of nail polish; roll it in your hands instead. This will stop air bubbles from forming. The best place to store your bottles of polish is in the fridge. The cold air will make the polish last longer.

Ariel

Follow Ariel for some swimmingly good beauty ideas!

Perfect Braids

Ariel usually wears her hair down. But for special occasions, she likes to braid it.

1 Part your hair down the middle. Take the front half of the left section and divide it into three pieces (or strands).

2 Use the three strands to make a braid: left strand over the middle strand, then the right strand over the middle strand, then the left strand over the middle again, and so on.

3 Keep braiding until just before you reach the bottom of your hair. Wrap a hair elastic around the end of the braid.

4 Now you're ready to braid the right section. Start from the front again and repeat steps 1–3. When you are done, pull both braids to the back of your head. Take out the hair elastics and fasten the two braids together with one hair elastic. Now you have the perfect braid.

Mermaid Locks

1 Brush your hair and pull the front section into a high ponytail. Secure it with a hair elastic.

2 Twist the ponytail around and around until it forms a bun. Secure the bun on the top of your head with hairpins.

3 Pull a small section of loose hair (about $\frac{1}{2}$ inch wide) from just behind the bun. Twist it around the base of the bun. Pin it in place.

4 Gather some hair rollers. Dampen all the loose hair and divide into small sections. Twist each section around a roller. Dry with a hair dryer.

5 Remove the rollers, but don't brush your hair. Pull one of the loose, curly sections up to the bun on top and wrap around the base of the bun, leaving the end of the curl loose. Pin it in place.

6 Do the same with all the curly sections. Alternate sides to keep the hairstyle balanced. To finish, twist some of the hair swirls, included in the beauty kit, into the base of the bun for decoration.

Nautical Nails

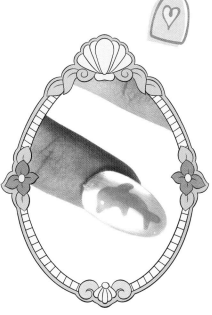

1. Paint your nails, or the press-on nails included in the beauty kit, with a clear base. Then paint a color on top. Use a color that reminds you of the ocean, like pale blue, turquoise, or silver. Let the nail polish dry.

2. For a starfish: paint a small dot of yellow polish in the center of the nail. Use a toothpick to drag the polish out to form five points. Let dry. Paint a smaller starfish shape on top with a darker color.

3. For a dolphin: use a toothpick to drag a dot of polish into points for the fins and nose. For the tail, dab on two smaller strokes of color using a toothpick. Add the eye with a tiny dot of white polish.

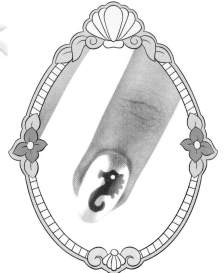

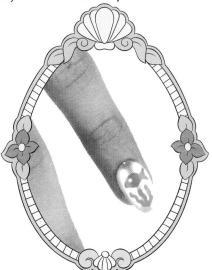

4. For a shell: drag a dot of your favorite color into a shell shape. Let dry. Paint a smaller shell shape on top with a darker color.

5. For a sea horse: use a toothpick to drag a dot of color into points for the nose, fins, and curly tail. Let dry. Add the sea horse's eye with a dab of white polish.

6. For a fish: paint a small, wide, oval shape, then use the toothpick to drag out the two points of the tail. Let dry and add an eye with white polish. To add seaweed, paint a small dot of green at the tip of the nail and drag it into three squiggly lines.

Snow White

"Magic Mirror on the wall. Who is the fairest one of all?"
Follow Snow White's beauty tips and it could be you!

Sleek Style

Snow White is lucky to have such beautiful dark hair that always looks so shiny and glossy.

1 Work a small amount of hair mousse through damp hair. Comb your hair back and then pull the comb from back to front in a large zigzag. Push the hair to each side of the zigzag and neaten it with the comb.

2 Use a large round brush and blow-dry your hair, curling the ends upward with the brush. Keep pulling the brush through your hair, up and out.

3 If your hair won't flip up, ask an adult to use a curling iron on the ends of your hair. Make sure the hair is curled in the right direction so it flips up and not under.

A Tip from Snow White

You may need to use hair spray to keep your style firmly in place. Be careful not to use too much. You don't want your hair to look more like a hat than a hairdo! Hold the hair spray can (or bottle) as far away from your head as possible before spraying it. For even better results, ask somebody else to spray your hair, standing about a foot away.

Romantic Ribbons

Why not add a pretty ribbon to your hair like Snow White? Brush your hair, being careful not to mess up the style. Then tie a ribbon around your head. Make sure the bow is on top.

Ultimate Updo

1 Make a center part. Fasten one side of your hair behind your ear with a hair clip.

2 Working with the loose hair, take a small amount from the front and twist it over and over, pulling it backward, so that it forms a neat twist close to your head.

3 As you twist the hair backward, gather up the next section of hair to add into the twist. Keep it neat so that the ends don't stick out. Work all the way to the back of your head. Then use a hair clip to hold the twist in place while you work on the other side.

4 Repeat steps 2 and 3 for the other side. Then unclip the first side, holding it tightly, and fasten both ends together with a hair elastic.

5 Lift up the ponytail and tuck it into the space between the two twists. Pin it in place. Now decorate the twisted sections of your hair with the hair swirls included in the beauty kit. Beautiful!

Gorgeous Gems

1 Apply a clear base coat to your nails. You can use the press-on nails from the kit.

2 Paint each nail bright red. If you make a mistake, dip a cotton swab in some nail polish remover to remove the polish.

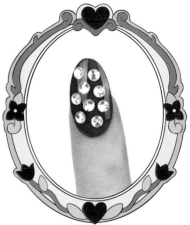

3 While the red polish is drying, add some nail gems in different patterns.

4 Or you could try placing just three gems down the center of each nail. If the gems are too small to pick up with your fingers, use tweezers.

5 When your gems are in place, carefully apply another coat of clear polish. This will help them stay on even longer.

Jasmine

Jasmine wants to show you how to transform yourself into a princess . . .
without the help of the Genie!

Jasmine's hair is unbelievably long and shiny, so she needs to take very good care of it. When taking Magic Carpet rides, Jasmine ties her hair back so it doesn't blow in her face and get tangled.

Princess Ponytail

1 Make a center part and divide your hair into two sections. Separate each side into two ponytails—one high on top of your head, and one low where your hair meets your neck.

2 Join the two back sections with a hair elastic.

3 Take one of the high ponytails, remove elastic, and loosely pull it back behind your head. Give it a twist and clip it in place while you do the same on the other side.

4 Next, remove the hair elastic at the base and join the two twists with the back section. Secure with a hair elastic. If your hair is long enough, add another elastic on a lower section of the ponytail. For an extra fancy look, wrap colored ribbon around the hair elastics.

Jasmine's Jewels

1 Brush your hair into a high ponytail. Keep brushing until every strand of hair is in your hand.

2 Still holding the ponytail, make sure it is as high as you want it to be.

3 Hold the ponytail in place with a hair elastic. You can use the flower hair elastic that comes in the beauty kit to decorate the base of the ponytail.

4 Twist in the shimmering hair swirls for a really dazzling effect.

5 You can also vary this look by leaving the back of your hair down and pulling the front half up into a ponytail.

Starry Nights

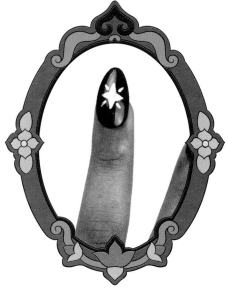

1 Paint nails with a clear base coat. Add a dark color and let dry. Then select a metallic color to paint on different celestial patterns.

2 For a sun: paint a small circle of yellow polish in the center of nail. Use a toothpick to drag the polish into the points of the sun.

3 For a star: on another nail, dab a dot of polish and drag it into a four-pointed star, using a toothpick. Add tiny lines around the star to really make it shine!

5 On your two remaining nails, simply dab on tiny dots of glitter polish, which is included in your beauty kit.

4 For a moon: paint a crescent shape onto another nail, using a really fine paintbrush or the point of a toothpick.

Perfect Pedicures

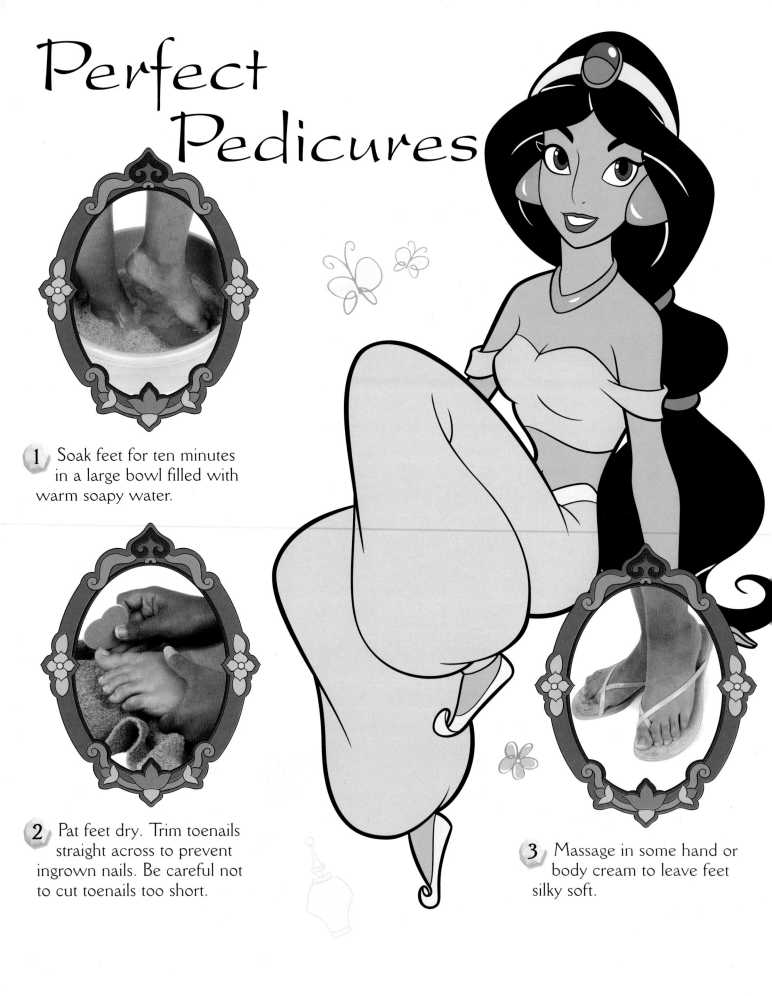

1 Soak feet for ten minutes in a large bowl filled with warm soapy water.

2 Pat feet dry. Trim toenails straight across to prevent ingrown nails. Be careful not to cut toenails too short.

3 Massage in some hand or body cream to leave feet silky soft.

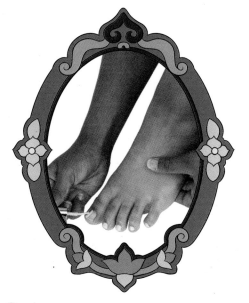

4 Paint each nail with a clear base coat, then let dry.

5 Apply a bright color, using three strokes of the brush (middle, then the left side, then the right side).

6 While the polish is still wet, carefully place one of the gems in the center of each toenail. Apply a clear coat on top of the gems.

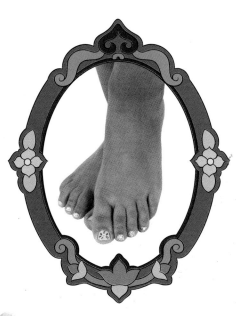

7 You can also add pretty patterns by using the nail stickers included in the beauty kit.

A Tip from Jasmine

Ask an adult to help you with your pretty princess transformation, if you find any of the steps difficult.

Cinderella

Cinderella looks beautiful even when she's doing her chores.
She can show you how to look like a princess
without a wave of a magic wand.

Cinderella's Secrets

When you wake up, you'll have a brand-new hairstyle!

1 Slightly dampen hair and divide it into lots of small sections, fastening with hair elastics.

2 Remove elastic and braid a section tightly (see page 15). Secure the end. (Pieces of yarn work well.)

3 Repeating step 2, braid the remaining sections.

4 Leave the braids in all night. In the morning, remove the yarn and shake out the braids. Your hair should be full of waves. Don't brush your hair—just run your fingers through it.

A Tip from Cinderella

For an extra-fancy look, add the hair swirls included in the beauty kit throughout your hair.

Sweet and Simple

Create new looks for your hair with these easy styles.

Gather your hair into a ponytail. Twist the ponytail close to your head. Pin your hair in place.

Scoop up hair into a high ponytail. Use the pretty flower hair elastic, from the beauty kit, to hold the ponytail in place.

Use two of the small flower clips, included in the beauty kit, to pull the front sections of hair away from your face. Try this with either a middle or side part.

Make a side part. Take the front section of your hair from each side and pull into a high ponytail, then secure with hair elastics.

Magic Before Midnight

1 You'll need some help with this style. At the back of your head make a horizontal part from ear to ear. Pull the top section of hair into a hair elastic.

2 Gather the bottom section of hair into a ponytail. Twist your hair downward. Then pull the bottom of the ponytail up and roll hair in. Fasten with hairpins.

3 Remove the hair elastic and brush the top section of hair in the opposite direction from your usual style. This will make your hair fuller.

4 Pull a small section of hair in front to frame your face. Twist the rest of your hair into a roll at the back; secure in place with hairpins.

5 Finish the look by adding the tiara that comes in the beauty kit.

Fairy Godmother
Fingernails

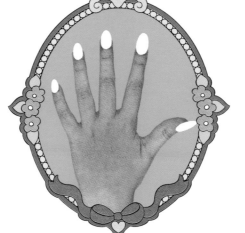

1 Paint a clear base coat on each nail and let dry. (Or you can use the press-on nails included in the beauty kit.) Add colored polish next—white is best for this design.

2 Before the white has dried completely, add a silver gem, from the kit, to the center of each nail. Let polish dry completely.

3 Using a toothpick dipped in silver or gold nail polish, draw eight thin star points around each gem.

1 Soak your feet in warm water for ten minutes. Add some scented bubble bath to help you relax.

2 Dry your feet, and massage with hand or body cream. Trim nails if necessary.

3 Roll the arch of your foot over the top of a wooden rolling pin or tin can. It's relaxing and good for your feet!

Rhapsody in Blue

4 Paint your toenails a pretty color to match your outfit. When the polish dries, add a coat of glitter polish, which comes in the beauty kit, for extra sparkle.

5 At night, rub your feet with more hand or body cream and put on a pair of cotton socks. Wear them overnight for silky soft feet when you wake up!

Paint your toes with a coat of pale blue polish over a clear base coat. Carefully add a musical note to the center of each nail, using a toothpick dipped in black, purple, or dark blue polish.

Sleeping Beauty

Hiding in the forest with the good fairies didn't stop Sleeping Beauty from taking care of herself. Follow her beauty tips and you can look as pretty as she does.

Once Upon a Dream

A reminder from Sleeping Beauty: Get your hair trimmed regularly to avoid split ends.

1 Brush your hair until it lies flat and looks shiny. If you have bangs, brush them forward, and push the rest of your hair back with a headband.

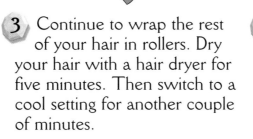

2 For curls, ask an adult to help you use rollers. First, wash and towel-dry your hair. Starting at the top of your head, wrap a 2-inch section of almost-dry hair around a roller.

3 Continue to wrap the rest of your hair in rollers. Dry your hair with a hair dryer for five minutes. Then switch to a cool setting for another couple of minutes.

4 Carefully remove all of the rollers but DON'T brush your hair! If you have bangs, brush them forward, then push the rest of your hair back with a headband.

Princess Style

1 Brush your bangs forward. Clip a section of hair just behind your bangs. You will use this section in step 3.

2 Take some hair from the back and brush it in the opposite direction from your normal style. This will make hair fuller.

3 Unclip the hair behind your bangs and let it frame the sides of your face. Place the tiara behind your bangs. This hairstyle will make you look very glamorous!

Heart's Desire

With or without the tiara, this hairstyle is perfect for a very special occasion.

You can also gather your hair into a ponytail and secure it at one side of your head with the rose hair elastic that comes with the beauty kit.

True Love's Kiss

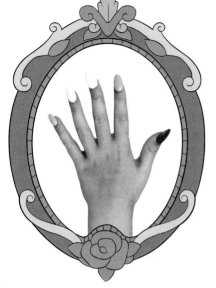

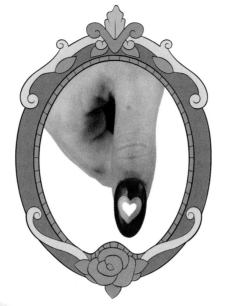

1 Paint each of your nails with a different color polish. Perhaps try red on the thumb, white on two fingers, and pale pink on the other two fingers. Let dry.

2 On the red nail, paint a lilac heart. Let dry. Then paint a smaller white heart in the center of the first heart. Next paint a red heart on a pink nail.

3 To make a heart, find a starting point about 1/4 inch from the top of your nail. With a toothpick, draw half a heart in the polish to the right. Then, go back to your starting point, and draw the other side of the heart on the left.

4 Paint a white heart on the other pink nail. On one of the white nails, paint tiny X shapes, using a toothpick dipped in red and lilac polishes.

5 On the remaining white nail, paint three lilac hearts. Add a clear coat of polish to all your nails, once they have dried.

Belle

Follow Belle's beauty tips and you'll be transformed
into a princess—no visit to the enchanted castle required!

Ribbons and Bows

During the day, Belle likes to tie her hair back. For special occasions, such as dinner with the Beast, she likes a fancier look.

Make a center part and gather all of your hair at the back of your neck. Secure with a hair elastic. Then tie a pretty bow with a ribbon.

For another elegant look, twist the sides of your hair toward the back before securing with a hair elastic and tying with a ribbon.

Fancy French Braid

1 Pull the sides of your hair to the top of your head. Divide your hair into three sections. Braid the left side, then the right side, over the center section.

2 Without losing your grip, gather another section of hair from the left side of your head. Braid the two together over the center section.

3 Repeat on right-hand side of your head, braiding the first section along with a new section over the center section.

4 Repeat this all the way down the back of your head, gathering new sections of hair from each side, as you go. Keep the braid nice and tight.

5 At the base of your head, braid the remaining hair as usual. Secure with a hair elastic and add a pretty bow.

A Tip from Belle

It may take a couple of tries to master French braiding. Remember— practice makes perfect!

Belle Goes to the Ball

1 Make a center part, then brush a small section of hair forward. You will use this hair later.

2 Now brush the back top part of your hair into a small ponytail, leaving some hair in the back. Fasten with a hair elastic.

3 Slowly twist the ponytail around itself. Guide the twists around the hair elastic to form a bun. Use hairpins to hold in place.

4 Now sweep back the loose hair from the front. Use the tiny flower clips from the kit to hold these strands in place, just below the bun.

5 For added sparkle, carefully place your tiara in front of the bun. It's the perfect princess look!

A Terrific Twist

1 Part your hair in the center. Make another part about 1/2 inch to one side to create a small section of hair.

2 Carefully twist this hair backward, keeping it neat. Use a large clip to hold hair in place.

3 On the other side of the center part, make another 1/2-inch part. Twist this section of hair as in step 2 and hold in place with the large clip.

4 Take out the large clip and secure each section with a flower clip. Keep twisting and securing sections of hair. Make sure the rest of your hair still flows freely down your back.

5 Gather the ends of the twisted sections into a ponytail at the back of your head. Fasten with a hair elastic, then twist into a bun, and hold in place with hairpins.

Pretty in Pink

1 A classic French manicure always calls for two colors of polish—white for the tips, and a very pale pink for the rest of the nail.

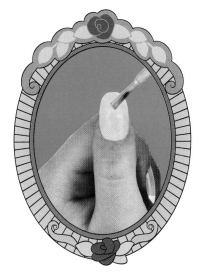

2 First, polish your entire nail in pink. Use three strokes on each nail: one in the center, then one on each side.

3 When polish has dried, paint a thin line with white polish at the tip of your nail.

4 When all tips have dried, add a final top coat with a clear polish.

A Tip from Belle

A French manicure will always make you feel like a princess!

Time to Go Home

The best way to stay beautiful and look like a princess is to get lots of rest, and to take good care of yourself. Here are some reminders from the princesses:

To remove your nail polish, dip a cotton ball in some nail polish remover. Rub the cotton ball over your nails, until all the polish is off. Wash your hands, and apply hand cream.

Never put a new coat of nail polish over an old color. A fresh coat always looks best.

◉ Rub hand or body cream onto your feet before bed so your feet are soft and smooth the next morning.

◉ If one of your nails breaks, fix it with a nail file, then file your other nails so they are all the same length.

◉ Before you go to bed, brush your hair. Never go to sleep with your hair pinned up or pulled back in a tight pony-tail, as this can cause damage to your hair.

◉ Even if you're really tired, always brush your teeth. Bacteria works overtime when you're asleep!

◉ If you want to keep your hair neat and tidy while you're sleeping, put it in a loose braid, or pull it into a loose, low ponytail.

A Tip from Cinderella

It's especially important to clean your hairbrush if you have fine, flyaway hair. Hair left in the brush will rub against your own hair, causing static, which makes your hair stand on end!

Absolutely Spotless

Try to clean your brush and comb every week or two. Comb all the loose hairs out of your brush and throw the hair away. Soak your brush and comb in warm, soapy water for a few minutes, then rinse. This will not only keep your brush and comb clean but your hair as well.

Neat and Tidy

When you dip the brush into the nail polish bottle, make sure the polish doesn't drip around the rim. This will cause the top to stick to the bottle and you may not be able to use that polish again!

How to Live Happily Ever After

It's much easier to look beautiful on the outside when you feel beautiful on the inside. So in addition to eating healthy foods, try your best to be a kind and generous person toward others.

Party Food

Eating healthy foods keeps your hair and nails in good condition. Iron is very important, so eat lots of leafy green vegetables and dried fruit. Red meat also contains iron. If you don't eat meat, make up for it by eating legumes (like chickpeas, beans, and lentils).

Positively Real

Cinderella always sees the best in everyone. This makes her beautiful on the inside as well as the outside. Try to find something nice to say about all the people you meet, even if you don't want to be best friends with them.

Say "Cheese"

Smiling is the best way to brighten up your whole appearance. Even if you aren't feeling very happy, try a small grin—it's amazing how quickly it will cheer you up.